THE DA VINCI QUESTION

James Emery White

InterVarsity Press
P.O. Box 1400, Downers Grove, IL 60515-1426
World Wide Web: www.ivpress.com
E-mail: mail@ivpress.com

InterVarsity Press® is the book-publishing division of InterVarsity Christian Fellowship/USA®, a student movement active on campus at hundreds of universities, colleges and schools of nursing in the United States of America, and a member movement of the International Fellowship of Evangelical Students. For information about local and regional activities, write Public Relations Dept., InterVarsity Christian Fellowship/USA, 6400 Schroeder Rd., P.O. Box 7895, Madison, WI 53707-7895, or visit the IVCF website at <www.ivcf.org>.

Design: Cindy Kiple
Images: Scala/Art Resource

ISBN 10: 0-87784-042-3
ISBN 13: 978-0-87784-042-8

Printed in the United States of America ∞

P 17 16 15 14 13 12 11 10 9 8 7 6 5 4 3

Y 19 18 17 16 15 14 13 12 11 10 09 08 07 06

There's something about Mary. (With apologies to actress Cameron Diaz, not *that* Mary.)

There's something about Mary *Magdalene*. Few religious figures have piqued our national curiosity more than Mary. She has prompted recent cover stories in *Newsweek, U.S. News & World Report* and *Time*. A Gospel in her name, unknown for fifteen hundred years, has supposedly been rediscovered. Rumors that she was a prostitute have been replaced with the claims that she may have been one of the earliest Christian leaders.

But most of all she is the force behind the bestselling novel (to date) of the twenty-first century, Dan Brown's *The Da Vinci Code*, which is now a major motion picture featuring the Oscar-winning duo of director Ron Howard and actor Tom Hanks.

So who is Mary Magdalene? What was the relationship between Mary and Jesus? Are there authoritative Scriptures other than the Bible (such as the *Gospel of Mary*)? Did Leonardo da Vinci leave secret clues about Mary in his art? Did the Council of Nicea invent the divine nature of Jesus for political reasons?

Many are puzzled by the claims of *The Da Vinci Code*. Is it fact or fiction? And what are the implications for the Christian faith?

The answers may surprise you.

WHO IS MARY MAGDALENE?

There are many women named Mary in the Bible. The best known is, of course, Mary the mother of Jesus. Then there is Mary of Bethany, who lived with her sister, Martha, and her brother, Lazarus, who was raised from the dead by Jesus. This Mary was the one who poured perfume on Jesus' feet and wiped it with her hair (see John 11—12). Neither of these women is Mary Magdalene.

It should also be noted that the unnamed prostitute in Luke (7:36-50) is not Mary Magdalene. In truth, we do not know who this woman was. In A.D. 591, however, Pope Gregory the Great delivered a sermon that *suggested* that Mary of Bethany, the unnamed sinner of Luke 7 and Mary Magdalene were all the same woman. He might have thought this since Mary of Bethany and the unnamed sinner were both noted for having wiped Jesus' feet with their hair. From that, it entered into traditional thinking that Mary Magdalene was a prostitute (see, for example, Mel Gibson's *The Passion of the Christ*). But the Bible doesn't say this, and the Vatican later made it clear that even though a pope first suggested it, it isn't right.

The Mary we are discussing is Mary *Magdalene*. Magdalene is not her last name; it designates where she was from—the city of

Magdala in Galilee. So in Jesus' time she was called Mary Magdalene.

This Mary had a rough history. Consider the passage where we first meet her in the Bible:

> Jesus traveled about from one town and village to another, proclaiming the good news of the kingdom of God. The Twelve were with him, and also some women who had been cured of evil spirits and diseases: Mary (called Magdalene) from whom seven demons had come out; Joanna the wife of Cuza, the manager of Herod's household; Susanna; and many others. These women were helping to support them out of their own means. (Luke 8:1-3).

This tells us that Mary Magdalene had been demon possessed and was delivered from that torment, apparently by Jesus. "Seven demons" often is symbolic for saying that her affliction was the most severe of situations.

Mary Magdalene was so grateful for what Jesus did for her that she devoted herself to his cause, giving of her time, service and financial support, and becoming part of his inner circle with the other disciples. She is mentioned fourteen times in the Bible, making her one of the most prominently featured women in the entire New Testament.

Mary Magdalene is included in many of the key scenes in the life of Christ, such as the crucifixion and burial of Jesus (John 19:25; Matthew 27:61). Perhaps most significant of all, she was the first witness *of* and the first witness *to* the resurrected Jesus (John 20). This is one of the prime examples of not only how Jesus honored Mary but more importantly how he elevated the role of women: During a day when women were not allowed as legal witnesses, Jesus first appeared to a woman, who testified to others about his resurrection.

THE *GOSPEL OF MARY*

In terms of the Bible, what we have already discussed is all we know about Mary Magdalene. But is there more to Mary's story? Some say yes, and it is this claim that has put Mary

Magdalene back into the spotlight, particularly through such books as *The Da Vinci Code*.

A document that began to circulate during the mid-second century A.D. claimed to be the *Gospel of Mary* (Magdalene). The author of this Gospel tells us that Mary was loved by Jesus above all women, that she was a leader among the apostles, and that Peter was threatened by her. Another writing that surfaced at the time suggests that Mary Magdalene was the companion of Jesus, intimating a sexual relationship—perhaps even marriage.

These ancient documents have been dated no earlier than the middle of the second century A.D.—some even later than that—thus their accounts are removed by decades from the actual life and ministry of Jesus, the apostles, and the formation of the church.

That they surfaced during the second century is accurate; that they were written by Mary is not. Though these manuscripts were not found until the twentieth century, they are not "lost" Gospels or "lost" books of the Bible.

Several of these manuscripts were discovered in an archaeological dig outside of Nag Hammadi in Egypt in the 1940s. The *Gospel of Mary* was also found in Egypt, but a few decades earlier. It actually showed up in a Cairo antiquities market in 1896 and was purchased by a German scholar. It was first published in 1955. We now have two Greek fragments of the *Gospel of Mary* from the third century, and a Coptic manuscript from the fifth century.

It is important to note that the people who knew about these manuscripts when they were first discovered rejected them as false documents. And the *Gospel of Mary*, along with such writings as the *Gospel of Thomas*, are still rejected by the overwhelming majority of scholars today. They are Gnostic documents written to challenge the growing Christian faith of the first centuries A.D.

Gnosticism was a movement during the early Christian centuries that claimed secret knowledge about Jesus, the world and salvation. These Gnostic ideas challenged the teaching of the newly established church. Decisively unorthodox and rejected by all the church fathers as heretical, the writings that the Gnostics claimed were genuine never took hold in the church.

And for good reason.

What the Gnostics claimed went against everything the early church stood for and what the witnesses to the early Christian movement knew to be true. For example, the *Gospel of Mary* denies the resurrection, argues against a second coming of Christ, and rejects the suffering and death of Jesus as a path to eternal life. The manuscript even says that there is no such thing as sin. People at the time knew this was diametrically opposed to what Jesus actually said, so the *Gospel of Mary* was never taken seriously. Just because this document surfaced again through archaeology does not mean we should give it the credence it never deserved to begin with.

Let's say that I wrote a book about Super Bowl XL. But instead of writing that the Pittsburgh Steelers defeated the Seattle Seahawks, let's imagine that I claim that my beloved Carolina Panthers stormed their way to the big game and beat the Steelers 34-3. In my book I cite all kinds of statistics, include play-by-play analysis, and then publish it as if it actually took place.

What would happen? Would anybody buy it, other than as a joke book for Panthers fans? Would anybody actually believe it? Hardly. As a credible account of Super Bowl XL, it would be laughed off the stands. Why? Because an estimated 141.4 million people watched the game in the United States alone.

That is why the early Gospels on the life, teaching and ministry of Jesus, written by those who were eyewitnesses, took hold. When the accounts written by Matthew, Mark, Luke and John came out, only twenty-five to fifty years after the time of Christ, people who had seen and heard Jesus were still living, and they knew whether the biblical Gospel accounts did or did not actually occur.

And the Gospels of the Bible weren't laughed out of the bookstores.

Not so with the Gnostic accounts that were written decades or even centuries later. They weren't suppressed by the church or emperor, as some have suggested; they were ridiculed. Simply because we uncover one or more ancient documents today, such as we did in the 1940s, doesn't mean they held any weight when originally circulated. That is why they were left out of the New Testament.

THE DA VINCI CODE

Beyond the veracity of the *Gospel of Mary*, there is the question of Mary Magdalene's relationship with Jesus. Was she simply a devoted follower of Christ or something more? Was theirs a sexual relationship? Did they marry and have children? It is this question that brings us to Dan Brown's bestselling novel *The Da Vinci Code* and the motion picture based on his book.

At first glance, the plot isn't anything that

stands out above the normal mystery fare: the murder of a curator at the Louvre in Paris leads to a trail of clues found in the work of Leonardo da Vinci and to the discovery of a centuries-old secret society. But as the plot unfolds, we find that the clues in Leonardo's work—and the mission of the secret society—revolve around the Holy Grail.

But instead of the Holy Grail being the chalice that Jesus used during the Last Supper, the novel suggests that it's the bloodline of Jesus.

The Da Vinci Code contends that Mary Magdalene was the wife of Jesus and the mother of his child. As she bore Jesus' descendants, and specifically a daughter named Sarah, Mary and her "line" became the Holy Grail. After Jesus' crucifixion Mary fled (with their child) to the south of France, where she established the Merovingian line of European royalty. This became the basis of a secret society that preserves Jesus' bloodline and protects the secret of the Holy Grail until the time is right to make it known to the world. Along the way, Brown also suggests that the church invented the deity of Jesus, and that all of these truths have been covered up, primarily by a secretive Catholic group known as Opus Dei.

Brown does not portray this as mere fiction. Before the first page of the story, he writes that his novel is based on fact, claiming that all descriptions of artwork, architecture, documents and secret rituals in the novel are accurate. He contends that there actually is a secret society that protects the Holy Grail, which has been in place since 1099, and that a discovery in 1975 in a Paris museum verified that its members have included Sir Isaac Newton, Botticelli, Victor Hugo, and Leonardo da Vinci. Brown also states that the Catholic organization known as Opus Dei practices brainwashing, coercion and "corporal mortification"—self-inflicted pain for the purpose of spiritual formation.

So this is not a mere novel. *The Da Vinci Code*

is a blend of fiction and historical assertion that suggests that the entire foundation upon which Christianity is established is false. Therefore, *The Da Vinci Code* deserves to be evaluated.

ABOUT MARY MAGDALENE AND JESUS

The Bible tells us that Mary Magdalene was a devoted follower of Christ, liberated from spiritual and perhaps physical torment that had plagued her life. She was present at his crucifixion and burial, and was the first person Jesus appeared to following his resurrection. The risen Jesus charged Mary to bring the news to his disciples, which she did. She was a remarkable woman, prominently featured in the New Testament and honored throughout Christian history.

In *The Da Vinci Code* a character of Brown's invention contends that this is not all that we know about Mary; she was married to Jesus, and the marriage is a matter of historical record.

Nothing could be further from the truth.

There is no historical record whatsoever supporting the idea that Mary was in a romantic relationship with Jesus, much less married to him. There is no evidence that indicates Mary had a relationship with Jesus beyond being a committed, devoted, spiritual follower. Karen King, a history professor at Harvard University and one of the world's leading authorities on Mary Magdalene, states categorically that there was no such relationship between Mary and Jesus.

So where did Brown get this idea? From *Holy Blood, Holy Grail,* a book that was published in 1982 and that the *New York Times Book Review* called one of the all-time classic examples of pop pseudo-history. And what was the source of *Holy Blood, Holy Grail*'s information? Neither the Bible nor ancient manuscripts, but French folklore.

What is the motivation behind such fabrications? Dan Brown himself has said on his website that he has a desire to promote the idea of the "sacred feminine"—goddess worship. One of the characters in the book says that "the quest for the Holy Grail is literally the quest to kneel before the bones of Mary Magdalene." In fact, the novel ends with the main character worshiping Mary Magdalene, seemingly experiencing her as a goddess.

ABOUT THE BIBLE AND ALTERNATIVE SCRIPTURES

What should we think about Brown's second major claim: that the Scriptures in the Bible are wrong? *The Da Vinci Code* says that the early church suppressed up to eighty alternate accounts of the life and teaching of Jesus, and then arbitrarily chose the four we have today.

Again, this is not true.

No scholar to date who has commented on Brown's novel has any knowledge of what these eighty Gospels might be. They simply do not exist. The four we have in the Bible are there because they were credible—both then and now; the Gospels of Matthew, Mark, Luke and John were universally affirmed as being authentic eyewitness accounts of Jesus' life.

What Brown is seemingly designating as alternate Gospels are the documents that circulated a century or more after Jesus' death, including the *Gospel of Mary*. Again, these writings have been dated no earlier than the middle of the second century, so they were far removed from the actual life and ministry of Christ, the apostles, and the formation of the church. They are not alternate eyewitness reports that competed with the Gospels of Matthew, Mark, Luke and John. They appeared decades, even centuries later, as attempts to challenge the clear teaching of Jesus.

ABOUT THE ART OF DA VINCI

One of the more intriguing assertions made in Brown's novel is that there are hidden messages about all of this in art, particularly in the work by Leonardo da Vinci. According to Brown, Leonardo filled his work with clues and signs pointing to Mary Magdalene as the wife of Jesus, mother of his child, and the Holy Grail.

The main work he focuses on is Leonardo da Vinci's famed mural *The Last Supper*, painted on a wall in the church of Santa Maria delle Grazie in Milan, Italy. Brown claims that in the painting the apostle to the right of Jesus is not the apostle John but Mary Magdalene.

Anyone who has seen da Vinci's great work, whether in person or through a reproduction in a book, agrees that the apostle John looks a bit feminine. Yet art historians have not concluded that da Vinci intended to portray a woman. During the Renaissance, it was common for artists to portray the apostle John as young, fair and clean-shaven.

It has also been observed that da Vinci had a tendency to portray all young men in his paintings in a feminine manner. Whether this was due to his alleged homosexuality or his personal stylistic taste, we do not know. But the claim that the image we thought was the apostle John is really a woman shows little understanding of Renaissance art, much less da Vinci's work.

Not only is the apostle in Leonardo's *The Last Supper* not Mary Magdalene, it was never intended to be construed as such. If there is any doubt about Leonardo's intent, it is proven by the existence of preliminary sketches for *The Last Supper* that Leonardo made of each apostle. (These sketches now reside in Venice.) Not only did he make sketches of each apostle, he labeled them. In his own notations regarding *The Last Supper,* the figure to the right of Jesus is labeled as John the Evangelist. And if the figure isn't John, as Brown contends, then where is he? No portrait of the Last Supper would leave him out.

Brown's novel also makes much of the fact that there is no chalice in the picture, claiming that Leonardo wanted Mary to be seen as the Holy Grail. Yet even the most novice of art historians have pointed out that there was no chalice present because da Vinci wasn't painting the moment when the bread and the wine were being passed. The scene captured in *The Last Supper* is specifically meant to capture the earlier moment when Jesus said that one of the apostles would betray him, not the institution of Communion, or the Eucharist, which would have featured the chalice. This is why we see the strong emotional reaction on all of the apostles' faces, including Judas's, which is shaded.

Because of these and other misinterpretations, Jack Wasserman, retired art history professor at Temple University, said that reading the book was nothing less than a trial. "I couldn't stand it. When you read a book and so much of it is nonsense, I just couldn't get from page to page without throwing a fit."

What about the secret society that supposedly included Leonardo da Vinci and such luminaries as Sir Isaac Newton, Botticelli and Victor Hugo? The documents attesting to the secret society, which were discovered in Paris in the 1970s, are believed by most to have been forged and planted there. The hoax was revealed in a 1996 documentary by the British Broadcasting Corporation.

THE DEITY OF JESUS

Throughout *The Da Vinci Code* there is much discussion about the nature and identity of Jesus. Brown has one of his characters state that "almost everything our fathers taught us about Christ is false."

Brown claims that the deity of Jesus—the idea that Jesus was God in human form—was created by the church out of thin air at the Council of Nicea (A.D. 325). Brown's novel argues that church leaders consolidated their power base by creating a divine Christ and an infallible collection of Scriptures, two novelties that had not existed before this famed gathering of Christian leaders.

To be sure, in the course of Christian history, few events were more significant than the Council of Nicea. The Roman emperor Constantine, recently converted to the Christian faith, gathered bishops from around the world to discuss a variety of issues. What the vast majority of Christians believed was without real debate. After all, the four Gospels of the Bible were already widely circulated, and they supported Jesus' claim to be divine.

Consider the following passages:

- "I am God's Son." (John 10:36)

- "I am the way and the truth and the life." (John 14:6)

- "The high priest asked him, 'Are you the Christ, the Son of the Blessed One?'
  "'I am,' said Jesus." (Mark 14:61-62)

- "Anyone who has seen me has seen the Father." (John 14:9)

Such statements did not constitute new teaching. They came from the mouth of Jesus himself. Robust conversation took place regarding the meaning and significance of Jesus' words; that Jesus said these things was never debated, never doubted, never questioned.

But during the first few decades following

Jesus, there was no churchwide statement or creed that captured the essence of Jesus' teaching. Why? For the simple reason that it was not needed. People were still close enough to the time of Jesus that it was widely known what he said and did. Further, the Scriptures that recorded it all—including the Gospels of Matthew, Mark, Luke and John—were widely available and referenced.

So why the gathering in Nicea? A challenge chiefly came from an Alexandrian theologian, Arius, who began to teach that while Jesus was a remarkable and exalted leader, he was not truly divine. The leaders of the church denounced this teaching, but Arius was determined to spread this new theology. And spread it he did, creating controversy in many churches in the Roman Empire. Constantine called all the bishops together to confirm what had always been taught and believed in order to confront the false teaching. Out of the gathering came the Creed of Nicea (which is very similar to what we know today

as the Nicene Creed), a statement clearly af-
firming the triune nature of God and the di-
vinity of Jesus. The language is ancient, and
even translated into English it reads a bit
awkwardly, but it clearly outlines what the
early church believed:

*We believe in one God the Father All-sovereign,
maker of all things visible and invisible;*

*And in one Lord Jesus Christ, the Son of God,
begotten of the Father, only-begotten, that is, of the
substance of the Father, God of God, Light of Light,
true God of true God, begotten not made, of one substance with the Father, through whom all things
were made, things in heaven and things on the
earth; who for us men and for our salvation came
down and was made flesh, and became man, suf-
fered, and rose on the third day, ascended into heav-
ens, is coming to judge living and dead.*

And in the Holy Spirit.

*And those that say "There was when he
was not,"*

and, "Before he was begotten he was not,"

*and that, "He came into being from what-
is-not,"*

> *or those that allege, that the son of God is*
> *"Of another substance or essence"*
> *or "created,"*
> *or "changeable"*
> *or "alterable,"*
> *these the Catholic and Apostolic Church anathematizes.*

The creed passed. And not, as Brown's novel contends, by a close vote. There were 300 or so bishops in attendance, and all but a handful signed the creed. Arius was branded as a heretic. Yet in *The Da Vinci Code* Brown puts Arius forward as the prime representative for Christian life and thought leading up to Nicea. Brown's characters claim that until that time, everybody thought like Arius, namely, that Jesus was a mere man, not divine.

The reality is that Christians overwhelmingly worshiped Jesus as their risen Savior and Lord, and every major Christian thinker and writer leading up to Nicea—from the original writers of the New Testament on through the early leaders of the church—

taught it with passion and clarity, including the New Testament authors Matthew, Mark, Luke, John and Paul; and the early church fathers Ignatius of Antioch, Justin Martyr, Irenaeus, Clement of Alexandria, Tertullian, Origen and Hippolytus.

The Council of Nicea invented nothing. It merely affirmed the historic and standard Christian belief, erecting a united front against those who would dilute or distort the life and teaching of Jesus.

CONCLUSION

The Da Vinci Code, even though a novel, presents countless other "facts" that are, to say the least, either exaggerations or outright falsehoods. For example, Brown claims five million women were killed by the Catholic church as witches. But even the most liberal estimates don't put the figure over thirty thousand—not to minimize the horrible nature of the witch hunts and trials. Brown grants great symbolic significance to the glass pyramid in front of the Louvre Museum in Paris, France, saying it is composed of 666 panes of glass. But this is not true. Due to the book's popularity, the Louvre staff actually counted the panes; there are 673. Brown also claims the Dead Sea Scrolls mention Mary Magdalene. In reality, they do not mention Mary Magdalene at all. The Dead Sea Scrolls date from 200 B.C. and don't have anything to do with Mary Magdalene (or Jesus).

I once read an interview of film director Oliver Stone when he was facing criticism for the distortions and factual errors in his films, particularly *JFK,* the faux documentary exposé on the Kennedy assassination. In a lecture at American University, he said that films shouldn't be the end-all for what is true. "[People] have a responsibility to read a book," he said, and then added that "[nobody] is going to sit through a three-hour movie and say, 'That's that.'" Sadly, he's wrong. That is exactly what countless numbers of people do. And when it purports to redefine the life and teaching of Jesus, it demands more inspection than ever.

When it comes to questions and concerns raised by books like *The Da Vinci Code,* or by any other medium—a film, a website, a television show—it is important to go to the sources and examine the truth claims. If someone makes a claim regarding what Christians believe or what the Bible says, it is important to determine if it is true. When we examine the sources and discover the truth about *The Da Vinci Code,* the word *fiction* must be applied.

The words of the apostle Paul remind us of the foundation on which we stand and by which all things must be judged:

> Evidently some people are throwing you into confusion and are trying to pervert the gospel of Christ. But even if we or an angel from heaven should preach a gospel other than the one we preached to you, let him be eternally condemned! . . .
>
> I want you to know . . . that the gospel I

preached is not something that man made up. I did not receive it from any man, nor was I taught it; rather, I received it by revelation from Jesus Christ. (Galatians 1:7-8, 11-12)

FURTHER READING FROM INTERVARSITY PRESS

The Gospel Code: Novel Claims About Jesus, Mary Magdalene and Da Vinci
by Ben Witherington III

ABOUT THE AUTHOR

James Emery White is president and professor of theology and culture at Gordon-Conwell Theological Seminary. He holds M.Div. and Ph.D. degrees in theology, history and biblical studies from The Southern Baptist Theological Seminary. He has also done advance graduate study at Vanderbilt University and continuing studies at Oxford University. He previously served as founding and senior pastor of Mecklenburg Community Church in Charlotte, North Carolina. He is the author of many books, including *Embracing the Mysterious God*, *Serious Times*, *The Prayer God Longs For* and *A Mind for God*. For information on Dr. White's speaking schedule, as well as his biweekly "Serious Times" update, visit www.serioustimes.com.